Counselling Young People in School

Counselling Young People in School

Guðrún Helga Sederholm
Translated by Anna Yates

Jessica Kingsley Publishers
London and Philadelphia

Originally published as: *Ráðgjöf í skólum: Handbók í félagsráðgjöf og námsráðgjöf* (1999)
Reykjavík: Háskólaútgáfan.

This edition published in the United Kingdom in 2003
by Jessica Kingsley Publishers Ltd
116 Pentonville Road
London N1 9JB, England
and
325 Chestnut Street
Philadelphia, PA 19106, USA
www.jkp.com

Library of Congress Cataloging in Publication Data
Guðrún Helga Sederholm, 1948-
[Ráðgjöf í skólum. English]
Counselling young people in school : a handbook on social work and student counselling / Gudrun Sederholm ; English translation by Anna Yates.
p. cm.
Includes bibliographical references and index.
ISBN 1-84310-044-4 (alk. paper)
1. Educational counselling--Handbooks, manuals, etc. 2. Educational counselling--Iceland--Handbooks, manuals, etc. 3. School social work--Handbooks, manuals etc. 4. School social work--Iceland--Handbooks, manuals, etc. I. Title.

LB1027.5.G8613 2002
371.4--dc21   2002028654

British Library Cataloguing in Publication Data
A CIP catalogue record for this book is available from the British Library

ISBN 1 84310 044 4

Printed and Bound in Great Britain by
Athenaeum Press, Gateshead, Tyne and Wear

Contents

About the Author

Guðrún Helga Sederholm is a student counsellor at the Sund High School (Menntaskólinn við Sund) in Reykjavík, Iceland. She graduated from the Iceland Teacher Training College (now Iceland University of Education) in 1969. After teaching for two years, she studied for a year at Denmark's Lærerhöjskole in Copenhagen, and then taught for two years in a Copenhagen primary school. On her return to Iceland, she taught at the Breiðholt primary/lower secondary school, and was head teacher at that school from 1976 to 1979. In 1985 she began studies in student counselling and social work at the University of Iceland. She graduated as a social worker in 1989.

In 1990 the Icelandic Ministry of Education asked her to undertake a development project on student counselling at compulsory school-age (6–16 years). Since 1991 she has been a student counsellor at the Sund High School.

In 1997 she was nominated to chair an ad hoc committee appointed by the Minister of Education on promotion of student counselling at all educational levels. The committee submitted its report in October 1998. Since 1993 she has taught school social work part-time at the University of Iceland.

Writings

Tvær Sögur af Stefáni [Two Stories about Stefán] (novel), 1979, Örn & Örlygur, Reykjavík. Published in connection with the UN Year of the Child.

Elías og Örnin [Elías and the Eagle] (TV play, dramatisation by Viðar Víkingsson) RÚV Icelandic National TV, 1989. Nordic competition.

Icelandic Film Fund Prize 1995 for a screenplay: *Bókabúðin Bifröst* [Bifröst Book Shop].

Two plays in a collection published by Mál og menning, *Leikum Leikrit* [Let's Put On a Play], 1998, Reykjavík.

Introduction

The aim of this handbook is to present the procedures I have applied in my work as a social worker and student counsellor in schools, both at the compulsory-schooling level and in high school, over a period of more than a decade. The purpose of this is, among other things, to provide useful information both to those who are beginning their careers as counsellors to young people, and to those who already have experience in the field. The handbook was written for practitioners who have been trained in counselling, such as social workers, student counsellors and psychologists, whose training is firmly based on scholarly and ethical standards.

The idea for the handbook arose partly from my teaching at the University of Iceland since 1993; I have taught procedures in school counselling, as well as supervising a number of students of social work and student counselling in work-training at the Sund High School. I have worked on development projects in student counselling for the Ministry of Education, have received many enquiries on procedure from working counsellors, and I have always felt a need to work systematically.

The procedures described here are mainly based on the so-called holistic approach, whereby the counsellor learns as much as possible about the client's circumstances in order better to understand the nature of the problem and the client's response to it. In addition, various theories of school counselling, and theories and methods of psychology, are described, concerned with specific problems. I have learned a great deal from the publications listed at the back of this book. While many of my sources are in Icelandic and Danish, and hence not accessible to most English readers, I recommend the English-language books, which have much to offer in the counsellor's work.

Methods in study counselling are described first, followed by the longest section of the book, on methods in personal counselling. And then two chapters on other aspects of the counsellor's work. The chapter on personal counselling is given the most weight, as I feel that good work in this field is enormously helpful to students in their study and work. This work is demanding, and must be based on good training of the counsellor, ongoing education, reflection, and systematic procedures that are in constant evolution. Student counselling is difficult, and does not yield the desired results unless the counsellor has a good relationship with the student. Mutual trust must exist, and school administration and teachers must understand the need for this.

Students at Icelandic high schools (such as Sund High School) are normally aged 16–20 years; schooling is compulsory from age 6 to 16, after which most youngsters go into further education of some kind. The age of majority in Iceland is 18, hence the older students are legally adults, while the younger students are still minors. This entails some difference in counselling practice.

Student counselling in Iceland is subject to the provisions of the Upper Secondary Schools Act no. 80/1996, and Regulations on the Staff and Organisation of Upper Secondary Schools, issued in 2001. The relevant provisions on student counselling in art. 9 of the Regulations are as follows:

Article 9

The school director shall appoint student counsellors in consultation with the school board. The student counsellor shall have completed studies in student counselling from a university, and be a qualified teacher or have teaching experience at upper secondary school level.

The student counsellor shall provide students with guidance on personal matters regarding their studies and the school. The counsellor shall judge whether the matter may be resolved with the school, or whether more specialised measures are required, from the relevant specialists or agencies. The counsellor shall communicate such information to the school director.

The student counsellor shall, among other things:

- organise and implement counselling on studies and careers in the school
- provide counselling on study and career options
- participate in organising various measures to promote the greater well-being of students in the school
- monitor the study performance of students who consult him/her or are referred to him/her, and propose improvements if necessary
- assist teachers with regard to study difficulties of individual students, and assist them in the organisation and supervision of student groups
- contact students' parents/guardians when necessary
- keep up with new developments in the field of student counselling
- prepare a report on work carried out at the end of each academic year.

Information acquired by a student counsellor on the personal affairs of individuals shall be confidential.

Referral and access to counsellors

Student counsellors visit all first-year (16-year-old) classes at the beginning of September and explain the nature of counselling: study counselling and personal counselling. New teachers are advised regarding certain danger signs in students' behaviour, of which they should take notice.

- Teachers may refer students to a counsellor.

- School management may draw attention to a student's circumstances, followed by consultation on a referral.

- Students may contact the counsellor themselves. This is the most usual course.

- Parents may draw attention to a student's situation.

- Friends of the student may draw attention to problems.

- Outside parties may make contact with the counsellor.

Students are ensured full confidentiality, and all parties are informed of this. Broadly speaking, counselling comprises study counselling and personal counselling, and the methods used vary according to the matter in question.

The methodology entails a holistic view of the student's circumstances. This means that the student is viewed as belonging to certain systems (system theory), i.e. family, friends, workplace, school friends, society, and so on. The objective is that counsellors should do their best to appreciate the child's circumstances, and strive to understand them as far as possible, while acknowledging their own limitations.

CHAPTER I

Study Counselling

Study counselling comprises many different functions:

- counselling on choice of school
- counselling on homework and study management
- counselling on choice of courses
- counselling students who have failed courses
- counselling students who transfer between schools
- counselling those who change to a new course
- counselling on choice of higher education
- counselling for career interest inventories
- career counselling
- counselling exchange students
- counselling for learning difficulties.

Counselling procedures at Sund High School

Counselling on choice of school

This involves visits by student counsellors to final-year pupils in compulsory education (aged 15), as well as parents' meetings, advice given on the telephone, and counselling given in the spring when prospective students register for the school of their choice. Visits to Sund High School by final-year classes in compulsory education are organised by student counsellors, together with the student association.

Counselling on homework and study management

This involves students visiting the counsellor once, or being invited to return weekly for four to six weeks for support. This means that a student file is opened: status in the various subjects is evaluated, failure to complete assignments is recorded, and students are asked to describe their working day. Schedules are used for this process. When students have considered the purpose of being in school, and together with the student counsellor have identified final study objectives, they are asked to write on the schedule how they feel they work best. Homework is generally estimated at two hours a day, with the exception of special assignments. If an assignment has to be completed, students are asked to enter the work involved in the schedule. Students are required to produce a schedule for a week at a time, and to bring it to the study counsellor at pre-arranged counselling sessions. The sessions are booked in advance, and if students cannot attend they must explain why, and book another session.

While this work progresses, all factors which hinder the student are examined. Planning aims to organise leisure time in a realistic manner, helping the student to work towards objectives, and to resist certain demands which hinder achieving set goals. A holistic view is taken throughout the process, and the possibility of learning difficulties is considered at the beginning of the process.

Counselling on choice of courses

First-year students (aged 16) receive guidance on choice of course in their regular lessons, as a special project. Students are also encouraged to visit the student counsellor and take a career interest inventory, which serves three purposes: to initiate discussion of the student's interests, to encourage thinking about higher education, and to compare the student's fields of interest with those of people in certain jobs. In this manner, efforts are made to encourage students to think systematically about which department is most likely to suit them and their interests.

Counselling students who have failed courses.

The day before the start of the autumn term, students who failed the first year, and who plan to take the first year again, are called to a meeting with the student counsellor, at which their position is examined. The focus is on the student's failure; they are encouraged to make use of their experience, with the help of the student counsellor, to ensure that history does not repeat itself. They are encouraged to contact the student counsellor on a monthly basis, to ensure that they study conscientiously, and avoid accumulation of problems.

Counselling students who transfer between schools

A considerable amount of counselling is provided to first-year students in October each year, following an assessment by teachers of their status in each subject. The teachers give the following assessments: good, adequate, inadequate, and unacceptable. Those students whose performance has been judged unacceptable in more than five subjects out of ten have their attention drawn to the advantages of the credit system applying in some other secondary schools, and they are encouraged to look into this. Students with reading difficulties are also encouraged to consider schools with the credit system. In such schools they can work at their own pace, and allow more time for subjects where they have difficulty. Students in the second to fourth year occasionally seek counselling because they are considering transferring to another school for various reasons.

Counselling students who change to a new course

In the autumn, after students begin their second year, a certain number of students visit the student counsellor because they are in doubt about the course they have chosen. A student who has taken a career interest inventory in the first year will be asked to bring it along. The matter of choosing a course is considered in light of the inventory. Grades are considered, along with other factors the student may have in mind. Students are encouraged to consider transferring to another course without delay, to minimise their problems in adjusting to a different curriculum. If more than the first half of the term has passed, each individual study subject is examined with them. The counsellor explains the extra study and tests that would be required in order to adjust to the new course.

Counselling on higher education

Fourth-year students are given a folder containing information on higher education, addresses, internet sites and various other sources of useful information. First-year students are encouraged at once to use books available in the school library on careers and study. Third- and fourth-year students have unlimited access to photocopied information on a wide variety of university-level studies, both at home and abroad. Students can borrow college syllabuses on short-term loan. Organised discussion of higher education begins in the first year, in connection with career interest inventories and study objectives. Counselling of this nature is provided in most counselling sessions. This discussion relates to important decisions about their future.

Counselling for career interest inventories

First-year students are encouraged to take the John Holland Career Interest Inventory (1973), and have the opportunity to compare their own fields of interest with those of 300 people in

400 jobs, connected with six fields of interest. Sessions of this nature comprise two parts, like other counselling sessions in the first year. The first half of the session is concerned with the inventory, while the second half is devoted to the student's personal views and circumstances. This gives the student an opportunity to mention worries and problems. The career interest inventories are often used as a 'way in' to the student counsellor. This method is an example of the holistic approach mentioned above.

Career counselling

This counselling is based to a considerable degree on career interest inventories and discussions with students during counselling sessions over the two or three years of consulting the student counsellor. The counsellor often assists students in making contact with companies and individuals working in the field about which the student is interested in learning more. These sessions include counselling about job applications.

Counselling exchange students

The student counsellor assesses in which year and course the exchange student should be placed, based on documents brought from the home country. This is generally carried out in collaboration with the head of teaching or the assistant head of the school. Exchange students are assigned weekly sessions, inserted into their timetable at the beginning of the school year, for about two months, after which they have monthly sessions with the student counsellor. Student counsellors strive to ensure collaboration with the student association to ensure that exchange students are able to participate in school social life. Meetings with host 'parents' of exchange students are arranged as necessary.

Counselling for learning difficulties

Counselling for students with learning difficulties has generally focused on students with problems in reading and writing. Organised work in this field did not begin in Iceland until the Iceland University of Education Reading Centre opened in the autumn of 1992. Assistance to this student group is still evolving. The Ministry of Education appointed a committee to deal with reading and writing difficulties in primary and secondary school. The committee produced a report in October 1997, which is an important guide for student counsellors, as it provides guidance on various measures and new points on service to these students.

Students with dyslexia are always at some risk of giving up on their studies and dropping out. Counselling them needs to be effective from the start, and it is necessary to defend their rights constantly, within the school and outside. Many such students have poor self-esteem because they experience constant difficulty in their studies, without having any reasonable explanation for their problem. Hence personal counselling to them is as important as study counselling.

Several years' experience in the Sund High School has revealed the value of having all new students take spelling tests at the beginning of the year. In collaboration with the student counsellor, teachers of the native language (Icelandic), who receive guidance on specific spelling errors made by students with reading and spelling problems, select and set aside test papers that may indicate dyslexia. The papers are sent to the University of Education Reading Centre for further processing. The centre carries out group tests of these students, and analyses their difficulties. Information is sent to the school's student counsellor, with guidance on the service required by the student. The reading centre offers students the opportunity to take individual tests in cases where severe reading disability is indicated; a fee is charged for this.

The school provides services to these students: extension of examination time, facilities to listen to the examination paper on tape, special assistance in examinations such as reading aloud of text, a special support teacher, oral examinations, and sessions with the study counsellor. The study counsellor provides counselling to students and their parents. Students who are diagnosed as having reading difficulties may borrow audio books from the Library for the Blind, for which they must show a certificate from the University of Education Reading Centre or from a specialist qualified to make this diagnosis, such as a neuropsychologist.

Recently, special services were introduced for students diagnosed with difficulties in mathematics: extension of examination times, and a support teacher who reads the questions to the student.

Students who have been diagnosed with learning difficulties comprise two groups: those with mild difficulties and those with severe difficulties. About 5 per cent of all students are diagnosed with severe difficulties. They are offered the option of taking the examination in a separate room with fewer students, and listening to the examination on tape. In the spring of 2001, the Ministry of Education made a grant to the Sund High School, to provide assistance to students who have severe learning difficulties. This funding was used to bring in a specialist from the University of Education, who gave a lecture to teachers of Icelandic on how best to provide support to students with learning difficulties. Courses were subsequently held for students.

Teachers of mathematics followed this example and brought in a special-needs teacher of mathematics to give a lecture on how best to provide support to these students. A course was subsequently held for the students.

Systematic work with these students is demanding, but it may be viewed as a contribution to reducing the drop-out rate from secondary school.

CHAPTER 2

Personal Counselling

Many students come to student counsellors because of personal problems. Study counselling often leads to personal counselling, in that students visit the counsellor to take a career interest inventory, or to express a lack of interest in their studies. In approximately half of all cases in which students consult the student counsellor, this leads to personal counselling. In personal counselling, records are kept on an individual basis. They are placed in a locked filing cabinet to which only personal counsellors have access. Matters dealt with in personal counselling are of many kinds; the main ones discussed later in this chapter are:

- lack of family communication
- loneliness
- suicide risk
- shyness and sense of inferiority
- depression
- examination anxiety
- eating disorders
- rape
- abortion
- pregnancy

- violence
- incest and sexual abuse
- homosexuality
- illness of student
- illness of family or friends
- substance abuse
- financial difficulties
- psychological and emotion trauma
- children at risk
- living alone.

Counselling procedures at Sund High School

A holistic view of the student's circumstances is crucial to personal counselling. The counsellor gets to understand the student's circumstances and needs, and applies professional knowledge in order to identify the problems and provide support and treatment. Students are promised full confidentiality in counselling, and thus their permission must be sought before teachers, school management or parents are informed of any situation. Attendance by individual students is examined as an indication of their well-being. They are informed that they are not being monitored; the counselling process is kept distinctly apart from any educational monitoring process. In professional counselling, monitoring is never compatible with a relationship of trust, hence the counsellor does not pass on to others any information on attendance, grades, or other information about the student.

The counsellor may refer the student to professional services, but in principle they book their own appointments. In serious circumstances, the counsellor will book an appointment for the student. The counsellor follows up on cases of students referred to specialist services, in order to ensure that the service is of benefit to them, and with regard to collaboration between specialist and counsellor.

Analysis of the student's problem is the major factor in personal counselling, and the basis of the entire procedure. The counsellor approaches the problem in a systematic fashion, examines all aspects of the student's circumstances, and gains an overall view. This clarifies the counsellor's understanding, and brings out the causative factors. This means in practice that if a student consults the counsellor about laziness or lack of concentration, the counsellor regards this as a symptom, not a cause in itself. Analysis can take two to three sessions.

Reports are written up after each counselling session. A file is kept on each student, in which session reports are kept, along with letters sent on the student's behalf: applications for financial assistance, doctors' letters, certificates, and so on. The report contains, for example, information provided by the student in the session, long- and short-term objectives, schedules, and projects assigned to the student. It is important for counsellors to have their own printer in the office, for printing out such sensitive confidential reports.

Counselling sessions are booked at the counsellor's office, and not via the school secretary. This is to ensure confidentiality: a student must be able to make an appointment with the student counsellor without the knowledge of other people. The maximum number of sessions per student is six, owing to the workload of the counsellor. Most counselling is carried out in October and March, and there may be a waiting list of up to three weeks at those times. Student counselling entails a considerable amount of telephone work, but it is important for counselling sessions not to be interrupted by telephone calls. Thus at Sund High School there is an arrangement with the school's switchboard operator. We also have a 'Do Not Disturb' sign available to hang on the door during counselling sessions.

Summary of principal counselling methods
INTRODUCTION OF COUNSELLING

Counselling is introduced to students in the first year. The objective is for them to get to know their counsellors, and know what problems they can bring to them.

ORGANISED COUNSELLING SESSIONS

These take place in October with new students at risk of failing, and in January with final-year students at risk of failing. The objective is to help them to change their study methods and deal with any personal problems that are hindering success in their studies.

FOUR-WEEK ORGANISED GUIDANCE

Students who seek help with problems managing their studies are offered a period of organised guidance. A card-index is maintained on students under guidance. Schedules are drawn up, and timetables are used. The objective is to teach students to manage their time, and work to a schedule to achieve their set objectives.

CAREER INTEREST INVENTORIES

Students are encouraged to take career interest inventories. The objective is for first-year students to gain insight into their own fields of interest, consider study and career options following graduation from secondary school, and establish a relationship with the counsellor, whom they can contact if problems arise during their time at the school. Older students are offered detailed counselling on study options and choice of career in connection with the inventory, and this gives them the opportunity to meet with a counsellor.

TWO-PHASE COUNSELLING SESSIONS

Sessions with students visiting the counsellor for the first time are divided into two phases. The objective is to consider the problem that has brought them to the counsellor, and in the other phase to gain an overall view of their circumstances, to ensure that their personal problems, and those that hinder them in their studies, do not go unnoticed.

ASSIGNMENTS

Students are given various assignments and projects in connection with solving their problems. The objectives vary: sometimes it is to motivate them and improve their decision-making skills; sometimes it is to allow the counsellor to gather information about a problem.

SCHEDULES

The counsellor and student draw up schedules, which are a means to solve a certain problem in a systematic manner. Examples discussed in the next section are: study schedules, financial schedules, schedules for setting boundaries, participation schedules, and session schedules. The objective is for students to gain the ability to understand the importance of looking to the future when setting objectives, and be able to assess their own success.

FOLLOW-UP

The counsellor follows up on cases that have been referred to specialists, and those which require long-term attention. The objective is for the student to remain in contact with the counsellor, and for the counsellor to have an overall view of the student's circumstances at any time.

Schedules

STUDY SCHEDULES

The counsellor and the student make a schedule for study over the next four weeks. This takes account of the student's leisure activities and work outside school. The schedule is written on an index card, and dates are included. Students tells their parents and teachers that they are meeting the counsellor once a week for the next four weeks.

The student attends the weekly counselling sessions to explain whether the schedule has been successfully kept to. If it has not, they discuss the obstacles preventing this. The schedule is revised if the original schedule proves impracticable. If it transpires that the student has personal problems, the method is changed to include dealing with those problems.

When students have attended four counselling session in four weeks, they are offered the opportunity of attending a monthly session with the counsellor.

FINANCIAL SCHEDULES

Students frequently have financial concerns. They may owe money on credit cards, or be in debt to banks or individuals. They may not be able to make ends meet. These worries affect their studies, and they may want to discuss the problems with a neutral party.

At a first session, the student and counsellor examine the financial situation: bank accounts, credit cards, cash, expenses of running a car, the student's accommodation, and other financial aspects. They examine the debts, and the student makes a summary of possible expenses – living expenses, rent and other 'fixed' expenses. Suggestions are made regarding a payment schedule, and the student is asked to write a schedule and bring it to the next session.

The student's schedule is then examined, and, if necessary, more practical solutions may be suggested.

The student attends counselling sessions once a week for five weeks, and the situation is evaluated on each occasion. Students are advised to tell their parents that they are seeing the counsellor in connection with their finances.

SCHEDULE FOR SETTING BOUNDARIES

Such a schedule is made with students who live with other people – their parents, friends, siblings – and with those who are trying to form a new social group after treatment for substance abuse, those who have a child, live alone or are cohabiting. The schedule is prepared on the basis of the individual, and the specific problem involved. Young people often have difficulty in setting relationship boundaries, and they may be insecure or subject to domineering behaviour or even oppression.

At the first session the situation is thoroughly examined, and the student's concerns are explored. Such concerns cause lack of concentration and anxiety, disrupting the student's studies. Students may be asked to note down the major factors on paper, and bring this to the next session.

An agreement is made on five sessions, and a schedule is prepared in accordance with this. The student is taught to say 'No', and that when saying no, there is no need to make excuses or explain. 'No' is a declaration of will, which should be respected. Body language and helpful forms of expression are discussed. The student is told how to gain control of a discussion, and what should be avoided.

The student is told that others are more likely to offer respect if clear boundaries are set, and that the opposite is true if others are always given way to. Self-respect is paramount. Projects are prepared, based on the student's own situation.

PARTICIPATION SCHEDULE

This schedule is primarily for those students who are isolated, lonely or reserved, but want to participate in social activities. This is also a preventive measure where there is a risk of suicide.

At the first session students are asked to draw up a network of relatives and friends. If a student has difficulty with oral expression, this is a very practical method. The network may be very sparse, and it can be alarming to see on paper how friendless an individual is. The counsellor must know how to work with this network, in order to help the student cope with the sad situation it depicts.

At the second session students are asked to talk about their interests. There are many clubs in the school, and the counsellor has a list of them and their leaders. Students are asked to consider whether they would like to join some club within the school. If so, the counsellor arranges a meeting between the student and the leader of the club, and attends the meeting to provide moral support. More often than not a connection is established, and the student participates in club activities.

If a student is not interested in clubs within the school, or has difficulty discussing interests, they are asked to describe to the counsellor when they were last really contented, to describe the circumstances and the people involved. This is a positive experience, and encourages further discussion.

Students are asked who they would like to get to know, and a schedule is drawn up on approaching the relevant person within a certain period.

COUNSELLING SCHEDULE

This form of schedule is made under various circumstances, but primarily to ensure the student's access to the counsellor.

A decision is made on the number of counselling sessions. The student attends counselling sessions once a week for five weeks, or less frequently, depending on the problem. The problem is defined, and a schedule is drawn up. The counselling sessions are entered in the student's timetable or personal diary. Ideally, sessions should be at a fixed time, as the student is then more likely to remember them. Students must let the counsellor know if they cannot attend because of illness or for any other reasons.

Such schedules are a standard feature of service to exchange students. At the beginning of the school year, they are assigned weekly sessions with the counsellor. After two months, if all is going well, the frequency of sessions is reduced to one every three weeks.

Students who have come from some other part of the country, and thus live alone, are also offered similar counselling schedules to those of exchange students, as are students who contact the counsellor at the beginning of the school year to notify an illness or other circumstances that call for regular counselling.

Laying the foundations
THE COUNSELLOR IS INTRODUCED

At the beginning of the school year the counsellor arranges with the supervising teachers of new students to visit each class, spending one teaching period with them. The objective is that the students should know who the counsellor is, and what service is being offered to them. It is important that 'Everybody knows who the counsellor is' in the school.

The counsellor's introductory session takes place in the context of a lesson with the class, in order to connect the work of the counsellor with the daily work of the school. The teacher is present during the session. Counsellors must take care not to become isolated in their interview room. They should take breaks at the same time as the teachers, and be visible in the school.

PRESENTATION AT A PARENTS' MEETING

At the beginning of the school year a meeting is held for parents of new students, to introduce them to the school. School administrators explain the school's work, curriculum, examination arrangements and students' obligations. Student counsellors explain the service they provide to students, and mention examples of how they deal with specific cases. They emphasise the fact that they represent students' interests. They give a brief summary of the last year's work, for instance the number of students who consulted the counsellor – how many boys and girls – and the nature of their problems in general terms.

The role of the counsellor at such meetings is important, because the counsellor is the member of school staff to whom students take their serious personal problems and difficulties relating to their studies.

Parents are more willing to seek advice from a person they have seen and heard. They have more confidence in them.

INFORMATION TO TEACHERS

The counsellor distributes to teachers, via their pigeonholes, information on things to watch out for in students, on student illnesses and other conditions, on dyslexia, and on useful reading and other sources. It is important for teachers to be aware of possible indications of students' problems. For example, they should note if a student does not attempt to communicate with others and appears to be isolated. They need to be aware of changes in appearance or behaviour, or difficulties developing in concentration, reading or writing.

There will be an information sheet regarding students with illnesses. These may be students suffering from chronic disease, epilepsy, or cancer, or students with conditions such as Tourette's syndrome, and students with ADHD. Such sheets are distributed to teachers only with the consent of the student. The student's name does not appear on the sheet, but it is suggested that the teacher contact the counsellor for further information. The sheet consists of two parts. The upper part deals with the disease, syndrome or disability, while the lower part comprises information the student wishes to impart to the teacher.

Also distributed in this way is information on reading analysis results from the University of Education Reading Centre for students suspected of being dyslexic. There will also be information material for teachers on useful reading, study findings, and meetings to be held by various groups, and information on projects (e.g. on bullying and substance abuse) that can be carried out with students within the class. Suggestions are also given for specific problems (e.g. better examination environment for dyslexic students and those who suffer from examination anxiety), or more generally for better conditions for study and rest within the school.

Principal subjects of personal counselling

Lack of family communication

Lack of communication in students' families is the commonest reason for personal counselling. Difficulties of this nature disturb concentration and lead to anxiety on the student's part. Students generally consult the counsellor initially on some other pretext: for example to take a career interest inventory, or to discuss homework problems, lack of concentration, or apathy. Many visit the counsellor specifically to discuss problems in their relationship with parents or guardians.

Parental authoritarianism is a common reason. Students feel that their views are ignored by their parents, that they do not listen. Because they are supporting the student financially, many parents feel they have total authority over the individual, and they may lay down rules the student is unwilling to accept – regarding study goals, future plans, money, their friends, and so on.

Another common reason for counselling is that parents make light of the student's problems and concerns such as an unhappy love affair, loneliness, suicidal thoughts, interests, and so on, and dismiss these as insignificant in comparison with their own concerns.

Indifference is another reason for students consulting the student counsellor. The parents may work long hours and prefer to have their leisure hours for themselves. The student may not have access to them, or may be reluctant to tell them about their problems.

Jealousy of siblings also occurs. The student may feel that the parents have a favourite among their children. Step-relationships, and divorce of the parents, can cause problems in the students' relationships.

These are the main subjects students wish to discuss with the counsellor; and, of course, anything else they feel unable to discuss with their parents. As mentioned above (p.25), counselling sessions with first-year students comprise two phases: the overt reason for the session is discussed in the first part, for instance a career interest inventory, after which the counsellor explores the student's personal feelings and circumstances. The student has the opportunity to mention any worries. This method is effective, working preventively, and strengthening the bond between the counsellor and the student. The number of counselling sessions in cases of this nature varies, but is generally not less than three. Sessions are held weekly. The counsellor normally suggests to the student that parents are informed that counselling is taking place because of domestic problems. In general, this alone will lead to the parents listening to their child. This is also a suitable means of giving pointers on parenting to the family. Following this procedure, parents often contact the counsellor to ask for a meeting. Almost without exception an acceptable solution is found for both parties – parents and child.

In order to reach a solution when there are problems in a family, the counsellor will hold a meeting with the student and parents, having obtained the consent of all involved. The student sits beside the counsellor for support and, drawing on points raised in previous sessions, the counsellor will state the student's wishes and why the student believes his or her parents' views should change. It is important for the counsellor to maintain control of the meeting throughout.

A goal is set at the beginning of the meeting and both parties agree to adhere to this outcome, with a further session to be arranged if it is not achieved.

It is always helpful to have access to a drawing-board of some kind for such meetings – the counsellor can then write up the main points raised, helping those involved to understand and remember what has been discussed. If the meeting is at a standstill or heading away from the goal set at the beginning, the counsellor can use the board to illustrate what is going wrong diagrammatically, showing the damage that the participants' attitudes are doing to communication in the meeting. This can be a turning point in negotiations, helping both parties to reach an acceptable solution.

The meeting means that action has been taken on a problem that everybody realised existed, but needed help to resolve. Parents are generally very pleased that the child had access to a counsellor with whom to discuss the problems.

Sometimes the communication problem cannot be resolved. In such cases the counsellor assists the student in applying for financial support to the local authority social services department. The counsellor writes to the department, explaining that the student would be better placed outside the home. If financial support is given, the counsellor becomes the student's supervising counsellor; these are the only circumstances under which a counsellor carries out both supportive counselling and monitoring of a student. As a rule, sessions are booked with a social worker or psychologist when an application is made for financial support because of domestic problems. The Reykjavík Social Services Department often authorises ten sessions. It is desirable that the counsellor and psychologist cooperate, in order to safeguard the student's interests.

Loneliness

Loneliness is a fairly common reason for seeking counselling. Teachers play an important role in such cases, and they may suggest booking a session for students who appear to be lonely. The information distributed to teachers on signs that a student may be unhappy has yielded good results, especially in cases of loneliness. Students may speak to the counsellor on their own initiative about being lonely. The counsellor arranges with the chair of the student association to draw up a list of all the different aspects of school extra-curricular activity. The counsellor arranges meetings between the leader of some particular activity and those who are interested in joining.

Experts are of the view that loneliness is a serious sign of possible suicidal tendencies, and thus great stress is placed on helping these students to bond with others. Assignments of various kinds have proved productive in work with lonely students. Counselling sessions usually number at least four to six. Experience shows that students make regular use of this service. Boys are in a majority in this group. Students who are lonely have often been subjected to bullying in other schools and are thus wary of their schoolmates. If students do not make friends in class, or find themselves in the same class as those who bullied them in their old school, the counsellor will suggest a transfer to another class.

It is important for teachers to be observant of relations between students, and contact the student counsellor if they become aware that a student is not fitting into the group or is subject to harassment. If teachers ignore such signs, serious cases of violence and bullying may result.

Suicide risk

The basic principle is that a person who claims to be planning to commit suicide should always be taken seriously. Students sometimes consult the student counsellor because they are concerned about a friend who has talked of suicide or displays signs of depression. It is important to reassure the student that the friend's trust is not being betrayed by seeking the counsellor's advice. The breach of confidence is carried out in order to seek the assistance of a professional qualified to deal with such cases. It is also important to make it clear to the student that no one should withhold such information; by doing so, that person becomes responsible for the other. Students readily understand this. They are willing to seek advice, if they have access to a counsellor.

A student who consults the student counsellor complaining of a lack of concentration, depression, anxiety, and a lack of interest in life, is at risk. Experience shows that it is important to ask directly whether suicide has been considered. The question is almost always answered instantly. If the student answers in the affirmative, it is important for the counsellor to apply a definite procedure.

Berit Gröholt, a Norwegian psychiatrist, visited Iceland in 1993 and gave a lecture to professionals on a procedure that has proved useful in such cases. Once it has been established that there is a risk of suicide, Gröholt recommends that counsellors make an agreement with an at-risk student:

- The student is encouraged to talk to friends or relatives.

- The student agrees to stay alive until a fixed day.

- The student is told the counsellor is ready to help change the student's situation, in collaboration with the student and his parents.

If the counsellor applies Gröholt's method, a relationship of trust is established with the student, who will be more likely to agree to the counsellor contacting a specialist, such as a psychologist, doctor or social worker. On occasion the situation is so serious that the counsellor will take the student to the specialist at once. Students at risk of suicide are ill, and receive medical treatment. Cooperation between physician and counsellor is important because the student spends long periods of time in school. The student also continues to visit the counsellor regularly for help in managing school work. If a student is admitted to hospital, it is important that he should not lose touch with the school; the counsellor liaises, and makes preparations for a return to school.

It is an invariable rule in such cases that the counsellor elicits the student's permission to inform the school's management of the situation. Students agree to this without exception, as they often require exemption from full attendance. Parents often contact the counsellor to express their gratitude for the help, as they had not realised the seriousness of the situation.

Preventive measures in this field are largely contingent upon teachers being aware of how their students feel, having a checklist of danger signs from the student counsellor, and reacting promptly when necessary to bring in the counsellor. The students must be familiar with the counsellor (classroom visits) and know that this is someone they can trust. It is necessary to follow up on students and their progress at school in such cases. This group includes individuals who are homosexual.

Shyness and sense of inferiority

It is quite common for students to seek counselling because of poor self-image. They may have low self-esteem, and lack confidence and courage. These are usually students in the younger age groups, and more often boys than girls. These problems often emerge in the latter part of two-phase sessions, or the subject may be directly introduced by the student. Numbers of sessions vary, but four to six is the rule.

SUICIDE – THE DANGER SIGNS

PRESENT SITUATION.

- Death of a loved one, violence, divorce, poor performance in studies, running away from home, bullying, breaking the law, pregnancy, doubts about own sexuality.

CONDUCT

- Isolation, reluctance to take part in social activities, weeping, prior suicide attempts, substance abuse, apathy, mischief, giving away worldly goods, clearing out.

PHYSICAL CHANGES

- Indifference to physical appearance, lack of stamina, not eating, not sleeping, low sex drive, fear of disease, depression.

THOUGHTS

- Suicidal thoughts, suicide plans, desire to get away, loss of rationality, narrow-mindedness, negative rather than positive thoughts.

EMOTIONAL CHANGES

- Boredom, apathy, emotional sluggishness, anger, guilt, pessimism, sense of helplessness, worthlessness, loneliness.

Students have generally experienced these problems for a long time. They may be quite desperate when they seek counselling, and hope for a quick solution. They are of an age when their interest in the opposite sex is at its peak, while they lack the confidence to make an approach. Worries of this nature lead to lack of concentration, and should not be underestimated. Counselling in such cases focuses on practical projects. These students want to take a step towards more self-confidence; they have had enough of 'good advice' that does not help them.

I call such practical intervention the 'step-by-step approach'. At the same time students attend weekly sessions with the counsellor, at which the project work is considered: what succeeded, what failed, and why. The objective is to pursue the project to the end. Students are pleased with this work, which they feel gives them more confidence and reduces their anxiety and shyness.

AN EXAMPLE OF THE STEP-BY-STEP APPROACH

An 18-year-old boy who is seeking counselling because he has difficulty concentrating on his studies. It transpires that he likes a girl who is the same age but in another class. He dares not approach her, lacks confidence, but would like to get to know her. The counsellor explains that there is a risk he will be rejected. He wants to take the risk, and the counsellor then explains the step-by-step approach.

Step 1: The counsellor suggests that during the first week he try to place himself at the margin of the group she belongs to – during recess, in the school corridors, at the bus stop. The objective is that she should notice him.

Step 2: At this session the counsellor and student discuss how things went, whether his self-esteem has improved, and whether he feels able to take the next step. He is ready to do so, and feels that he is now in a better position, as he dared to come closer to her. The counsellor suggests that during the second week he approach her more closely in the group and try to make eye contact with her from time to time.

Step 3: The student is again asked to assess the results of the past week, and he says that she has now often looked at him. He is pleased with himself, and wants to continue. He does not feel able to address her directly, but the counsellor suggests that he participate in talk in the group as far as circumstances permit.

Step 4: Results are evaluated, and the student is pleased with what has been achieved. He has entered into discussion in the group several times, and the girl clearly noticed him. Also his name came up during the discussion, so she now knows his name. The counsellor suggests that he phone her at home to ask her to the cinema, because it is often easier to take rejection on the phone than face-to-face, if indeed 'no' is the answer. The student feels that he is more confident than before, and does not feel that rejection would affect this. He feels that he has learned a method that he can apply in other circumstances, and he is ready to make the phone call. The counsellor prepares the student for the next session being his last session for the time being.

Step 5: The final session is concerned with examining the results of the method with regard to whether the student has gained more confidence. He is content with himself, as mentioned in the fourth session, and was successful when he phoned the girl. She was friendly, and he says he surprised himself when he was talking to her. He felt able to talk to her about all sorts of subjects.

A confidence scale is often used at the beginning of the work, especially with those who have difficulty expressing themselves about how they feel, and their emotions. Priority is placed upon explaining that confidence varies from one person to another, and that shyness can run in families. It is also important that the student understands that miracles cannot be expected, and set realistic goals and objectives.

Depression
Mention was made above of the fact that the counsellor does not regard laziness or lack of concentration as explanations but as

symptoms of a condition requiring further attention. This means that when a student consults the counsellor complaining of these symptoms, a careful examination is made of the underlying causes.

A student's school history is considered, and an attempt is made to pinpoint when these feelings began to affect studies. The counsellor asks the student about sleeping habits, work habits, relationships at home, financial matters, sexual experience, and other factors which may serve to explain the situation. Excessive or irregular sleep, problems falling asleep or waking up, restlessness, anxiety about studies, a tendency to put off studying, and isolation from friends may indicate depression, especially if the examples the student is asked to give indicate that the situation has existed for some time.

Parents often seek help with problems of this nature.

It is important for the counsellor and student to establish a good relationship. It is often useful to ask the student to keep a diary for a while, so that with the counsellor they may gain a better understanding of the problem. Students who are in doubt about their sexuality exhibit the same symptoms. Sessions are generally not fewer than one to two a week for two to three weeks, in order to diagnose the problem and establish a bond.

The counsellor refers these students to specialists – psychologists or psychiatrists – and suggests to parents who ask for help on such matters that they seek specialist advice. If the conclusion is that the student is depressed, or clinically depressed, a doctor will normally prescribe medication, and sessions are arranged with a psychiatrist or psychologist. Collaboration between specialists and counsellor is important, so that the school's requirements of students will be consistent with their state of health, and in order to maintain contact if a student has to be admitted to hospital.

Such cases are followed up, in order to ensure that the student receives service that is beneficial. Students who are being treated for depression or other psychiatric problems have a regular monthly session with the counsellor, or more often if the specialist regards this as desirable. The counsellor always asks the student's permission to inform teachers of the student's illness, so that necessary exemptions can be granted without any problems. Such permission is almost always given.

Examination anxiety

Many students consult the student counsellor about anxiety before examinations. Counselling sessions soon reveal whether they suffer from 'normal' examination nerves, or whether they are among those students who suffer from debilitating examination anxiety.

The first group receives counselling that is mainly concerned with explaining that it is natural to feel nervous when one faces difficult and personally important tasks. Students are given guidance on how to reduce their examination nerves, while learning to live with them.

Those whose examination anxiety is of a debilitating nature attend four to six sessions, at which systematic efforts are made to teach them relaxation techniques and the degree of anxiety is evaluated.

The relaxation techniques are based on hypnotic relaxation; the student meets the counsellor once or twice a week for relaxation. The relaxation process takes about 30 minutes. The method (described below) is explained to the student, who is told that it is not always successful, but that if the relaxation technique is practised at home as advised, between counselling sessions, it is likely to prove beneficial.

- The student sits in a comfortable chair with arms, and is taught abdominal breathing. This is a way of using the abdomen, not the chest, and leads to greater relaxation of the whole body, which is important in relaxation. This is explained to the student.

- The student is asked to concentrate on the breathing with eyes closed. The counsellor speaks in a hypnotic voice.

- When the counsellor sees that the student is breathing deeply, the relaxation can begin. The student is told to concentrate on certain parts of the body, from head to toes, while the counsellor deepens the relaxation by emphasising the heaviness of, for example, arms and legs. The counsellor always speaks in the same hypnotic voice, and observes the student's breathing. Exhalation is used to deepen the relaxation.

- The counsellor goes through the process of relaxing the body twice, and tells the student to exclude negative thoughts, and relax and enjoy the moment in complete security.

- At the end of the process, the counsellor says that the student will be 'woken up' by counting down from five; on reaching the number one, the student will wake up gently, well rested and carefree.

It is explained to the student that it is natural to feel fatigue after such relaxation – that this is a good sign, and indicates that the relaxation was successful. This is repeated at counselling sessions as often as is deemed necessary, usually limited to a maximum of five times because of busy working conditions.

The view is taken that such severe examination anxiety is rarely an isolated phenomenon, hence some students are referred to specialist services. These students are allowed extended examination time, and they may take their examinations alone in a room. They are also offered the opportunity for a relaxation session with the counsellor just before the examination. The last feature has been very successful. These students generally maintain contact with the counsellor throughout their four years at the school. The objective is to provide students with extensive service initially, gradually reducing the supportive measures in order to prepare them for a different study environment, and less support.

If two or three teachers state that the student's performance is affected by problems with examinations, the student is allowed extended time in end-of-term examinations. It is important that students and teachers realise that extended examination time cannot be granted unless the problem has been assessed by the student counsellor. There is great demand for this provision, and the conditions must be clear to both teachers and students.

Eating disorders

In cases of students with eating disorders the student counsellor is generally approached by friends of the affected person. Family members may also contact the counsellor and express their concerns, and teachers seek advice regarding students who they believe have an eating disorder. It is rare for a student with an eating disorder to initiate a consultation with the counsellor to discuss the problem.

Eating disorders are a hidden problem, and the individual in question does not realise that a problem exists. The counsellor seeks a means of approaching the person cautiously so that the relationship will not be disrupted. On occasion the problem is very severe, in which case the counsellor makes contact with the parents and calls them in for an interview to explain their responsibility and to point out the importance of seeking expert advice without delay. In such cases, students often defend themselves by denial, so the counsellor informs the parents that the progress of the case will be kept under review. The counsellor often recommends a specific specialist, and consults on the best approach regarding teachers' behaviour, the school's response, and study plans. If the student is admitted to hospital, the counsellor visits the student to maintain the connection with the school, in consultation with the specialist treating the student.

When the counsellor has confirmed that the student has an eating disorder, and the student accepts the fact that the counsellor 'knows' what is happening, hostility will often be shown to the counsellor, who may be regarded as one of the enemy. Counsellors must thus deal with a difficult situation. A typical scenario might unfold as follows.

> Some girls talk to the counsellor about a friend's problem. They are very concerned that she eats nothing and is very thin. They are afraid she may be anorexic. The counsellor explains to them how the girl will be approached and praises them for having drawn attention to the situation. The girls do not want it known that the problem was first mentioned by them.

> The counsellor contacts the girl's class teacher and discusses the progress of her studies in general terms. The teacher states that she is generally a good student, but that there are concerns that the student hands in work irregularly and late. She is never happy with her work, although she gets good grades. It generally emerges during the interview that the teacher is concerned about the student's health, and is pleased to have the opportunity to discuss this with the counsellor. They agree that the counsellor will call the student in for an interview.

> The student attends the interview. It is obvious that she is very thin. The session begins by the counsellor telling her than she has been called in because the teacher is concerned about her being unhappy with her work, and handing in work very late. This leads to discussion, revealing more information, which the counsellor applies when the girl is asked directly whether she has an eating problem. The girl is eager to talk about food,

and soon the discussion progresses to her family. The next session is booked.

The counsellor continues discussion of the food problem, and asks the student to say exactly what she has eaten during the past two days, and what she weighs. It is confirmed that she may be anorexic, and the counsellor tells the student that she must be kept under observation as this is a very grave problem. She gives her permission for the counsellor to speak to her parents. Had she not given permission, it would be explained to her that her parents would be contacted anyway.

The parents are asked to attend an interview at the school, where the counsellor's view of the situation is explained. They agree that it is difficult to get their daughter to eat, and that they are very concerned but do not know what to do. The counsellor gives them the name of a doctor and offers to book an appointment for them, as time is of the essence. They agree. The counsellor asks them to get back in contact immediately after they have seen the doctor.

The girl becomes very hostile to the counsellor and 'forgets' to attend counselling sessions. The counsellor goes and fetches her out of class. She is angry with the counsellor for interfering. The role and responsibility is explained, and they decide to meet once a week.

The parents do not contact the counsellor, who calls them, and asks what has happened. It transpires that they did not like the doctor, and do not intend to go again. The counsellor explains to them the responsibility that it incumbent on them, and asks them to keep a diary of what their daughter eats over the next week. They agree. They agree to call the counsellor in one week.

Sessions with the student go well, and the counsellor focuses on establishing a relationship of trust.

The parents call. It transpires that the girl has lost weight, and has eaten almost nothing. The parents agree to go back to the doctor, and it is decided that their daughter will go with them.

The parents call again. The girl has been admitted to hospital, where she will stay for several weeks. The counsellor tells the parents that he will be in touch with the social worker at the hospital.

The counsellor makes contact with the social worker at the hospital, and they decide that the counsellor will meet the student regularly at the hospital, in order to maintain the relationship.

Rape

Students who consult the counsellor about rape often do so at the urging of friends or family. They come to take a career interest inventory, or to discuss lack of concentration, laziness, poor organisation, relationship problems at home, possible depression, and so on. They are usually reluctant to discuss the real problem, the rape. They have a damaged self-image, generally have low self-esteem, and they often feel life is not worth living. Many have sought specialist help for depression or other psychiatric problems, but have not been able to bring themselves to discuss the problem, or the specialist has not been responsive.

Such cases are often 'old' in the sense that some time has passed since the event took place. The person may attempt to 'forget', or hope that the pain will gradually ease. When the question of the rape has been uncovered, the counsellor offers to contact a rape crisis centre. The student generally agrees to this, and the counsellor makes an appointment on behalf of the student. Follow-up is important in such cases, and the student requires considerable support when she seeks help. On occasion a student may attend an interview at a rape crisis centre, but then inform the counsellor that she will not go back. She feels that it does no good. At such times, support is important, and may be crucial. In most cases the student agrees to return to the centre, when the actual work can begin.

In connection with trips made by groups of students, serious instances of rape may arise, when other people have observed the assault without intervening. Such cases are especially difficult; rape is a highly traumatic experience, and especially so if others have watched. In general such cases are carefully 'hushed up' for a time, but friends ultimately seek help for the victim. The victim feels an overwhelming sense of shame, and perhaps guilt for having been drunk. When the victim has come to the counsellor and faced the experience with the counsellor's help, much work remains to be done. The victim may not be willing to bring charges against the rapist, and may have very mixed feelings toward those who stood by and watched. The knowledge that her schoolmates know what happened can be difficult. The student must be enabled to work through these problems, and it may take two or three sessions to persuade the student to seek specialist help.

Abortion

Both boys and girls consult the counsellor regarding abortion. The majority are girls, who are seeking counselling about a possible abortion. By the time they consult the counsellor, they have generally made up their minds, and intend to have an abortion. They are primarily seeking practical information on where to go, and want confirmation that they have made the right decision.

The counsellor examines the situation with them, and if their decision remains unchanged at the end of the process, the counsellor explains what to do, where appointments can be made, and what happens at the hospital. The counsellor encourages the girl to tell her parents about the abortion. In some cases the girl is entirely opposed to this, in which case the counsellor provides whatever support can be given. She books an appointment with a social worker at the hospital, and offers the girl counselling sessions after the procedure.

Cases arise in which girls have had abortions without any support from anyone, and later seek counselling because of unhappy and guilty feelings.

On occasion, boys consult the counsellor regarding a girlfriend possibly having an abortion. They sometimes seek help with feelings of guilt over an abortion that took place some time ago. In such cases they tend to be isolated and cannot discuss the matter with their friends. This underlines the importance for students to know that the counsellor is always ready to give counselling and support. As already described, students first hear of this in the first year, when they enter the school: the counsellor visits the classes, explains how counselling works, and mentions the 'sensitive' issues that students can discuss.

Pregnancy

Cases of pregnancy are relatively rare in secondary school. A few cases arise each year, especially in the final year. A number of these girls opt to continue with their pregnancy.

The girls consult the student counsellor to discuss their pregnancy, and relations with the father of the child and his family. Counselling focuses on finances, the upbringing of the child, organisation of studies, examinations, relations with parents, and so on. Expectant fathers also consult the counsellor to discuss their relationship with the mother of the child. The counsellor discusses the families of both, finances, relations with friends, and custody of the child. Cases are of various types: expectant parents who are provided with accommodation in the home of his or her parents; expectant parents who rent a flat of their own; those who cannot live together, or do not want to; and pregnant girls who are on their own.

The first group receives counselling on becoming a family, on living in the parental home, the grandparents' involvement in care of the child, the importance of parents' standing together and sharing responsibility in bringing up a child, changes in their social life, and finances. Those who rent a flat of their own receive similar counselling, but with more emphasis on finances and on workload in school and in employment. The cases of those who cannot live together, or do not want to, are more complex, and it is important to offer support. In most such cases, counselling is given. The parties are under emotional strain. The same applies in the case of pregnant girls on their own. They are under great emotional stress, uncertain of their future, and they are concerned about unclear relations with the father of the child, in addition to having concerns about their studies and about financial matters.

The counsellor provides all those involved with information on their rights via social security authorities, and benefits available through the local authority.

Violence

Counselling regarding violence is mainly concerned with violence in the home, which unfortunately some students are subject to. Most commonly it is the father of the family who subjects others to physical violence or mental cruelty.

The two-phase counselling sessions with first-year students specifically examine relationships at home. The student has the opportunity to express concerns, which may include information on violence. In the case of a student aged under 18 who is a victim of violence, the counsellor has a legal duty to inform the authorities (see pp.61–62 'Children at risk').

Oppression gives rise to problems with communication: an individual is not allowed self-expression. Such children grow up in an atmosphere of concealment, repressed by the person in control or the violent person. The spouse of the violent person may try to keep relations in the family under control, in order to avoid provoking more violence. This is the same pattern as in the families of alcoholics. The family is in denial, and the members of the family are, to a greater or lesser degree, emotionally stunted, as the interests of the perpetrator of violence are always given precedence. Denial becomes a part of life, because people do not feel able to face the true situation.

Students are reluctant to talk about the home situation, and they feel guilty about discussing their family with a stranger. Experience shows that if the counsellor is conscious of this, and shows understanding, mentioning this at the start and returning to it at subsequent sessions, it is easier for the student to discuss the problem.

In such cases the counsellor tries to persuade the student to have the parent who is not violent (it is usually the mother) come to an interview. In most cases she does so, and in general the student counsellor is the only outside person she can talk to. Interviews with the spouse of a violent person are difficult, and it is vital that the counsellor respect the person and her standards while making it clear that the purpose is to safeguard the interests of the child. Often 'mothers' counselling' develops into discussions of divorce or radical changes in family life, and support must be given during this process. The counsellor recommends the mother to a women's refuge, women's counselling service and other resources, depending on the nature of the problem. It transpires that all the mothers want the situation to change, but they need considerable help to make this happen. The women are often overcome with feelings of guilt over their acquiescence, and the effect of this on their children. Specialist help is required, and they are given information on where to seek it.

The student attends regular sessions where there is an opportunity to express anger towards the violent person, and, equally, the constant sense of guilt. The number of sessions varies. If the situation at home is unchanged, the counsellor provides information on social supportive means that would enable the student to move out, or helps with getting the assistance of relatives who may, for example, offer a place to live. Sometimes the very fact of the student moving out will change the domestic situation.

Students may consult the counsellor with regard to violence in cases of bullying. If the perpetrator or perpetrators are in the school, the counsellor calls them in, one at a time, and gives them the opportunity to discuss the bullying. In general, bullies have problems themselves, and they are offered counselling for a time in relation to these. It is made clear to them that the bullying will not be tolerated. The counselling provided to bullies almost always leads to the cessation of bullying.

An important aspect of the effort to eliminate bullying consists of projects prepared by the counsellor for all first-year classes. These are generally projects on ethical themes and the rights of the individual, and they include both individual and group work. The projects are completed and handed in anonymously to the teacher. The projects are intended to take about two teaching periods. The first period is spent completing the projects, and the second in discussion. Students have the opportunity to consider their own status, and that of others, in the class.

The counsellor processes the project results, and makes a summary of findings, which are discussed with the teacher. If problems exist in the class, or in relation to individual students, they jointly prepare an action plan.

Incest and sexual abuse

It is relatively rare for a student to seek counselling over incest or sexual abuse, but it occurs from time to time. The problem is generally brought to light when the student and counsellor have established a relationship for other reasons, such as lack of concentration, apathy, depression, anxiety and irregular sleep. In many cases the person has been subjected to sexual abuse in childhood, and into the teens, with the problem having festered for a long time, preventing the student achieving goals in study and private life.

Experience shows that a rape crisis centre is a good solution for girls. The student counsellor books an appointment at the rape crisis centre, establishing a personal bond from the start. Appointments are also made with specialists accustomed to dealing with such cases. Follow-up is required, and the counsellor provides as much support as the student needs. The girls often drop out of school while they are working through their problems, as they are under enormous stress when they succeed in unleashing their anger towards the abuser, often after many years of repression. The family may even be broken up, because the abuser is often a close relative. On occasion, the family may refuse to believe the girl, and turn against her. This period of working through their feelings is very difficult for the girls and they require considerable support. The counsellor asks the girl's permission to tell school authorities about the problem, in order that the school may make certain allowances and exemptions to prevent the student from dropping out. It is important that the girls and the counsellor draw up a schedule for study and attendance, as the school is sometimes all they have to hold on to.

In the case of boys, it is more difficult to initiate the process. Boys are reluctant to admit that they have been sexually abused, and will strive to 'deal with it themselves' indefinitely. Thus it is important that a bond be established between counsellor and student, so that the student knows that he can 'open up' the case to the counsellor. Boys who have been sexually abused appear to be at special risk of substance abuse. Sometimes they consult the counsellor over problems with substance abuse, confrontations with teachers, and problems with their studies, in which case the counsellor begins with these matters. The counsellor always opens the way to discuss more painful issues. There is some risk of suicide among those who have been sexually abused, and this is discussed in counselling sessions. Boys may be referred to specialists, in which case the counsellor helps them book an appointment. the counsellor refers them to specialists who have proved effective in similar cases. Follow-up is the rule in such cases. It is necessary that counsellor and specialist collaborate.

Homosexuality

As in many other cases of personal counselling, students seek counselling because of unhappiness at school or in their private life. Reasons may include lack of concentration, laziness, depression, anxiety, relationship problems at home, isolation and suicidal thoughts.

In the two-phase sessions with new students, sex is one of the subjects discussed. The student understands that sex may be discussed with the counsellor. People often find it embarrassing to discuss sex, yet it is a driving force of most people's lives. Young people are fascinated with sex, and student counsellors must feel able to discuss it frankly. If they cannot do this, there will be major 'blind spots' in their counselling. All young people have drives and desires that must be satisfied in some way. If they cannot it causes them worries, unhappiness, anxiety, lack of confidence and other feelings that make life difficult. The counsellor must be prepared to respect different views of sex, and different desires and drives.

Homosexuality tends to be well concealed until the late teens. Experience shows that if students are given the opportunity for frank expression about their sexuality, and they accept the advice to contact a gay organisation, this immediately makes them feel better. To come out as a homosexual to parents, siblings and the family is very difficult. Students require support and encouragement from the counsellor. A method that has proved successful is for students to draw up a schedule on how best to do this, as well as attending regular counselling sessions, to discuss their experiences, expectations, fears, and their own prejudices and those of others. Homosexuals naturally tend to focus on prejudices against them, but in order to change anger into understanding it is important that they examine their own prejudices. The counsellor offers to answer any questions parents may have, if they wish to make contact. Discovering that their child is homosexual is often a major shock to parents, who initially feel unable to discuss the matter with friends, but feel it is important to be able to talk to the counsellor.

Illness of student

When the student counsellor visits classes of new students entering the school, they are told that it is important to inform the school if they have any disease such as epilepsy, diabetes or other chronic ailments. They are also urged to tell the school if they have impaired hearing, vision, and so on.

The student normally visits the counsellor to give such information. The supervising teacher is advised to encourage students, in private interviews with them, to do so. The counsellor asks the permission of the student to tell other teachers of the problem.

In the case of chronic disease, the counsellor prepares an information sheet on the disease for teachers. This is a leaflet in two parts, which the student has an opportunity to read before it is distributed to the teachers. The first part of the leaflet briefly describes the disease, and the second part is about the person who has the disease, and the service required. The student's name does not appear; the student is identified verbally to the teachers. The leaflet is placed in the teachers' pigeonholes, and they contact the counsellor for further information. This system has proved effective. Counselling sessions with students with diseases are every two months. Other sections deal with counselling for students with mental problems.

Illness of family or friends

Students are encouraged to seek counselling if a member of the family or a friend is ill. In general the illness causes them anxiety and disrupts their daily life.

Many students seek counselling because a member of the family is an alcoholic, which has an influence on the whole family. In addition to attending regular counselling, it is suggested that they contact Al-Anon or other organisations dealing with alcoholism. Many booklets on the subject are available, and it is important for these to be available to the student.

A student who has a parent who is dying may seek counselling; or if the counsellor becomes aware that a student's parent is seriously ill, the student may be contacted with an offer of counselling. This counselling is quite complex and person-centred. The main objective is for the student to have the opportunity to discuss the problems with a person outside the family who can provide professional advice. Students may find it difficult to discuss matters of this nature with friends, and thus they tend to feel alone with their problem. It is often necessary to grant exemptions and make allowances for them with regard to examinations, attendance, and so on. The counsellor generally asks the student's permission to tell the teacher of the problem. Students make good use of this counselling.

Worries about friends are no less difficult for young people than for their elders. Students often seek counselling for this, mainly to express their worries and to try to identify the problem. They feel some responsibility for their friends, and they wish to help them. These counselling sessions comprise professional counselling and information provision, in addition to reinforcing the bond between counsellor and student, so that students knows they may come back to discuss the development of the problem with the counsellor at any time. Problems are of various kinds: the student may be worried that the friend has an eating disorder, is an alcoholic or has a psychiatric disorder, for instance.

Substance abuse

This is an extensive and difficult field for the counsellor. Many schools are establishing their own policies on prevention of substance abuse. Student counsellors are intended to participate in policy-making, together with other staff and management. This entails meetings and gathering of data, and allowance must be made for this when the work is planned.

Substance abuse increases year by year, and the use of illegal substances is now rising fast. It is important for the counsellor to have the possibility of substance abuse in mind when analysing the problems of those who seek counselling, and that questions are asked about drink and drugs once a bond has been established with the student. Students normally answer such questions frankly, but in the case of considerable use of drink or drugs, they initially tend to minimise the problem. Hence it is important for the counsellor to give the student sufficient time to form a bond. In small steps, the counsellor establishes the connection between substance abuse and the disruption of the student's daily life, until the student has, after a number of sessions, gained a more realistic view of the problem.

Assistance provided to students with a substance-abuse problem varies. The objective is to persuade the student to decide to stop the substance abuse. A few options are available, and the counsellor gradually explains them to the student in counselling sessions. When the student as decided what to do, the counsellor can offer help, for instance by booking an appointment at an alcoholism/addiction facility. The counsellor may accompany the student to the first appointment, if the student so requests. If the student goes into a treatment programme, the counsellor is the contact between student and school, and after treatment the student attends regular counselling sessions.

If the student is not prepared to take any action regarding the substance abuse, and does not believe that it does any harm, the counsellor takes no action if the student is over 18 (i.e. an adult under Icelandic law). If the student is under 18, the parents are contacted and offered advice.

The counsellor prepares a schedule of counselling sessions for the student. This schedule, which is always accepted by the student, serves two purposes: to maintain contact between counsellor and student, and to make clear to the student that the counsellor sees that there is a problem. A schedule of this nature plays an important role, and yields results: against the tendency for substance abuse to increase with time, the bond with the counsellor may prove vital.

It is important for the counsellor to maintain regular contact with the local police. Interviews with the police are arranged every two years in order to seek information about developments in the drug world, information that can also be passed on to others. It is also important that the counsellor arrange for the police to visit first-year classes each year. Representatives of the police give a presentation on substance abuse to teachers approximately every three years. Experience has shown that teachers tend to underestimate the problem and are grateful for such information sessions.

The student counsellor should gather information for parents, which is distributed to a meeting of parents of first-year students in October each year. Hard-hitting comments against substance abuse on posters displayed in the school, in collaboration with teachers, are very effective. The experience of the police shows that drug dealers may be found among students, and they dislike seeing these comments. They know that someone knows what is going on, but not who, and this seems to reduce sales within the school.

Students often come to the counsellor because they are concerned about a friend's use of drink or drugs, and want to discuss what can be done. They receive counselling on their behaviour towards the friend, setting boundaries, co-dependency and other related matters. Students are urged not to undertake responsibility for a friend's health by concealing information. Parents, too, often ring the counsellor for information and advice.

Financial difficulties

Students may come to the counsellor because they feel unable to continue their studies because of financial difficulties. This problem may emerge in sessions originally concerned with some other matter, hence it is important that the counsellor gain an all-round view of the student's circumstances.

Reasons for students' financial difficulties include the following: the student may be an orphan, the parents may be unable to give support, illness of the student, or serious relationship problems in the family.

The role of the student counsellor is first and foremost to serve the interests of the student. When counselling sessions reveal financial difficulties, the counsellor must discuss possible resources with the student, and give support in gaining access to them. Social services departments can make study grants to students; they are subject to monitoring, which consists of submitting their grades after half-yearly examinations. These students receive support from the counsellor at school. The counsellor writes to the relevant body, explaining why financial support is required, and the student approves the application. In some cases students have gone through very difficult experiences, in which case the counsellor may feel that sessions with a social worker or psychologist would be beneficial, and asks for ten sessions in the application for assistance. Cooperation between the counsellor and the specialist is important so that the student gets better personal service and the counsellor has a holistic view of the case. The student attends regular counselling sessions during the period of financial assistance.

More than half the students in Reykjavík upper-secondary schools work part-time, and their needs vary. Some find themselves in debt, and seek counselling to help them gain control of their finances. In such cases the student visits the counsellor weekly for some weeks, and pays off the debt according to a schedule prepared at the first session. The situation is regularly reviewed, and this method usually proves effective. Many students live alone, and need help in financial management. The objective of such counselling is to prevent the student from dropping out.

The student counsellor assists students in applying for maintenance payments from a parent where relevant, and in making any other form of application for financial support.

Psychological and emotional trauma

The student counsellor draws up a plan on response to trauma, which may be applied when students suffer trauma. It is important that the school have such a plan, as this will ensure the correct response, and not a random approach in the heat of the moment.

The cause of trauma could be, for instance, a natural disaster, traffic accident, other accident, suicide, or death from disease. The student counsellor plays a key role when such trauma has occurred, and collaborates with parties inside the school and outside. When a natural disaster or other mass accident happens, the counsellor checks whether any student or member of a student's family is among the victims. The counsellor visits classes, and discusses response to grief with the students, and provides guidance on how to behave towards the bereaved person. Counselling is offered to close friends or others who react strongly to the news. Death always leads to emotional strain. The strain is particularly great on those whose circumstances are otherwise difficult. A student who loses a close relative receives trauma counselling for four to six sessions; the same applies to students who have suffered other trauma, for example an unhappy love affair, rape or violence.

Trauma counselling is based on a fixed procedure created, tested and reviewed by the counsellor. The following examples are of procedures in the case of a student's death, and where a student has lost a close relative.

TRAUMA PROTOCOL FOR THE DEATH OF A STUDENT

- The counsellor and school administrator confer on response to the trauma.

- The administrator informs teachers of the situation and the planned response.

- The counsellor speaks to the deceased student's classmates and gives them advice regarding appropriate response.

- The school administrator holds a ceremony in memory of the deceased, together with the students.

TRAUMA COUNSELLING FOR BEREAVEMENT

- The counsellor contacts the student who has suffered trauma.

- Counselling sessions are booked.

- The counsellor discusses the main aspects of grieving with the student.

- The counsellor prepares the student for the funeral.

- The counsellor prepares the student for returning to school.

- The counsellor contacts the student's family, and specialists if applicable.

- Several weeks follow-up, comprising sessions with the student and teacher.

Family members often contact the student counsellor to provide information on trauma suffered by the student. The counsellor then immediately approaches the student to offer help. Collaboration with clergy and with specialists may be helpful in such cases. In many cases, people ring the counsellor at home. The counsellor provides teachers and other school staff with advice on how to behave toward students who have suffered trauma.

Children at risk

In cases of domestic violence, students often express concern about violence inflicted on their younger siblings. Students have difficulty in discussing such matters. The counsellor handles this with care, acknowledging the strain for the student in talking of this problem.

When a counsellor is aware of any kind of violence against children under 18, by law, and without exception, the local child protection authorities in the community where the victim lives must be informed. It may take two to three sessions to prepare the student who has provided information on violence against a sibling for the matter to be notified to the authorities. It must be explained to the student that it is vital that the circumstances of the victim be changed, and that it is the right thing to do to reveal the violence. Feelings of guilt and fear are experienced when the student has told of the violence. The counselling process comes into conflict with the way the child has been raised, in that the violence has been hushed up and the violent person has been shielded, while the children grow up knowing that they must not provoke the perpetrator, for fear of the consequences. There is a great fear of change. Students also feel a sense of relief, as they have generally kept concerns to themselves and have not been able to discuss them with the non-violent parent. It is a strain on the student to hear the counsellor explain in broad terms the characteristics of violent people and their families. The counsellor will often sense withdrawal, – a desire to postpone notification and 'see if things improve'. Thus it is important for counsellors, from the beginning of their counselling careers, to face up to being able to deal with cases of children at risk, and give notification to the authorities. If a counsellor is in doubt, advice must be sought. The same applies in cases of alleged neglect of children and adolescents.

Students also come to the counsellor to discuss violence in their own group, for example when a student is subject to gross bullying, or if there is a power struggle in progress in the class or in a group of youngsters. They sometimes feel coerced by their classmates or others, who may insist that they drink alcohol or use other substances in class parties when they have no wish to do so. Care must be taken in intervening in classes to try to encourage the students to get to know one another. Young people in high school have the right to choose their own friends, without feeling embarrassed about not participating in all the class's activities.

Living alone

Some students live alone in a rented flat or room. These students have access to counselling on such matters as rights, finances, nutrition, cleanliness, and so on. They also have access to counselling on setting boundaries vis-à-vis their friends, social life, drink and drugs, and employment, in addition to general student counselling.

Some of these students are lonely and do not have friends at school, hence it is important to put them in touch with the school's social activities, and book regular counselling sessions, which are entered on their timetable twice a month. They value having fixed sessions, and their attendance is good.

Other students may be too caught up in social life, and find themselves in difficulty with managing their homework due to constant visits and phone calls. Financial problems may also arise. These students are counselled by organising a plan for a week at a time, and have fixed counselling sessions while they work according to the plan. The greatest problem is visits by friends at all hours. The counsellor prepares a plan for setting boundaries in consultation with the student, who is taught to follow it. Most students are fairly successful with this, unless there is a problem with substance abuse. If this is the case, the counselling takes this into account. A financial plan is made, and reviewed weekly.

Students who share a flat often find themselves in conflict with their flatmates. Sometimes it is necessary to call the flatmate in for an interview, and an agreement is reached on solution of the problems that have caused conflict.

CHAPTER 3

Counselling and the Wider School Community

The student counsellor has many different responsibilities, among which is to provide services to people other than students. This takes place in interviews, at meetings, by letter and on the telephone. For example, it is important to make it clear to teachers, school administrators and other staff that the authorities, and parents, must be informed if they become aware of some legal offence regarding a student aged under 18. This applies, for instance, to drug use and dealing, violence or prostitution. In broad terms this aspect of the counsellor's work may be divided into three categories:

- parents
- teachers
- administrators.

Counselling and parents

As stated in the previous chapters, parents contact the counsellor in various contexts. The student's right to confidentiality should always be respected, and parents at Sund High School are informed that, without the student's permission, it is not possible to discuss the content of counselling sessions. On occasion parents try to influence the counsellor's advice to the student: 'You tell her to stop seeing that boy.' Parents also tend to feel that they have a right to know what has been discussed in counselling. If it is clarified to parents that students' confidence will not be breached, as it would be contrary to their interests – turning them against both counsellor and parents if they feel 'ganged up' on – it is possible to achieve excellent collaboration with parents. Parents generally understand perfectly well that personal relationships are based on mutual trust, and that it is preferable that they be carried on face to face. They appreciate that the counsellor is safeguarding the child's interests, and that his role of counsellor is primarily to help them communicate better by enabling them to trust each other. To teach them to start talking again.

Parents are given some counselling on parenting: parents are taught to respect boundaries, to respect the child's views, to learn to trust and change their manner to the child, to name but a few aspects.

Many parents of younger students (16–17 years old) have difficulty in respecting the child's boundaries on such matters as tidiness of the child's room, friends, homework times, the child's earnings, and so on. Parents often feel that their boundaries on these matters are the only boundaries.

Some parents do not respect their child's views, feeling that what the child says is 'childish' or 'not interesting'. They do not provide any opportunity for exchange of views, as they feel this is beneath their dignity. They are the breadwinners, and support the child financially, hence their views must be the right ones. This is a power struggle that unfortunately often ends with strained relations, and undermines the child's self-image.

Some parents see the world as a place of constant danger for the child, due to drug pushers, alcoholics and violent people, and feel that the child must be protected, while others are more insouciant, saying 'There's nothing I can do, anyway, so I interfere as little as possible in my child's life'. Of course, parents generally love their children, and it is a good idea to explore this at the commencement of counselling, at the same time as explaining the counsellor's role as spokeperson for the child. This means that both wish to safeguard the child's interests. Parents understand this, and agree, and become more receptive to counselling. It is easy to explain to parents that authoritarianism, negativity, disparagement and nagging will lead the child to withdraw from them and stop trusting them. This also entails the risk that the child will start concealing important matters from the parents. Most parents also understand that children have certain obligations in the home, and must respect certain rules, like other members of the family. Parents are allowed to set boundaries. If parents are offered the opportunity to meet with a counsellor, they generally do so. This is in itself a precaution against strained relations.

As stated before, the student counsellor collects information on the signs and consequences of substance abuse, and this is distributed at a meeting with parents of new students in October. Parents seek information of this kind and make good use of it. They contact the counsellor if they have suspicions in this direction.

If the students and counsellor feel it would be useful to invite parents to a meeting at the school, this is done. Parents contact the counsellor when a student is ill. The counsellor makes a plan with the parents, student and school on how to conduct the studies.

If a student is seriously ill or in danger of some nature, parents can meet with the counsellor at school. In cases of substance abuse, rape, loneliness, depression and other serious matters the counsellor will often get in touch with the parents, usually after checking with the student that it is all right to do so.

Students are encouraged to tell their parents that they are in counselling. This alone tends to open the way to discussion of other matters, and the student's circumstances generally improve. This tells the parents in clear terms that the child is becoming an adult, and one who has a spokesperson.

Cases arise from time to time of parents wishing to discuss their own personal affairs, for instance in cases of divorce or illness. The counsellor points out that he is primarily a counsellor to the students, and amicably suggests that the parent seek counselling elsewhere, though a recommendation to a specific specialist or institution may be made at the parent's request.

Counselling and teachers

Student counsellors do a great deal of work with teachers, and it is important for the student that relations between teachers and the student counsellor are good. At Sund High School the counsellor provides the first-year's supervising teachers with advice regarding supervision classes and assignments related to them, and suggests ideas on preventive work. The counsellor teaches the supervising teacher the basics of interview technique and discusses the nature of short interviews (7–10 minutes).

With the student's permission, the counsellor provides teachers with information on students (as described in previous chapters) in cases of illness, learning difficulties, and so on. Teachers also seek advice regarding individual students, and point out students about whom they have concerns. They seek counselling regarding problems with discipline in class, students' lack of interest, and problems of communication. In many cases the counsellor produces an assignment for the class to complete, in order to gather information and objectify the problem.

Assignments can be of many different kinds according to the circumstances; the following example is concerned with a problem of discipline in class.

The class does not obey a certain teacher, and repeatedly complains about him to the class's supervising teacher and to the school administration. The situation is serious.

The counsellor prepares an assignment, which school administrators show to the teacher. The objective of the assignment is for the students to express themselves anonymously; they are also required to propose ways to improve the situation, both with regard to themselves and the teacher.

The counsellor prepares the assignment and administers it to the class, explaining that she is the students' spokesperson, and that the completed assignments will not leave her hands. She also explains that after processing the findings she will come and discuss them with the class, and that the school administrators will discuss them with the teacher.

THE ASSIGNMENT QUESTIONNAIRE

The student states his/her gender.

- What is your status in the class?
- Who do you think is the leader in the class?
- Is there a power struggle between individuals in the class?
- Do you find it easy to put your views to your class-mates?
- Do you think that any students are given the cold shoulder by their classmates?
- What is the teacher's status in the class?
- When the class will not listen to the teacher, what does he do?
- What do you think he should do?

- What can students in the class do to improve the situation?

- What can you do to improve the situation?

Generally such a process is useful, provided that school administration is favourably disposed towards it. Students' proposals are often highly conservative in nature; for example in a case like the one described, they may suggest that the teacher imposes penalty points on students, and expels them from the class when they reach a certain number of points. I feel it should be said that teachers who have difficulty in imposing discipline often have trouble in following up on their threats; they tend to patronise the students, and are nervous with them. Guidance from an experienced teacher can often be beneficial.

The counsellor also produces assignments with the objective of paving the way for discussion of study objectives, and means of attaining them. The counsellor visits classes at the request of supervising teachers, to discuss management of homework, working hours, and so on.

The counsellor produces an information pack, which is distributed to final-year students, on study options after graduation from secondary school, containing information on addresses and websites of various universities and other institutes of higher education. The information pack also contains details of study loans and grants for which students can apply. In connection with distribution of the information packs, the counsellor arranges with teachers to visit the classes and talk to students.

Students in danger of failing their final examinations are called to see the student counsellor, in consultation with the supervising teacher, soon after the New Year. They are offered regular sessions to help them manage their studies better and pass their exams. Students make good use of this service, especially if teachers are supportive and encourage them to attend counselling.

Teachers, like other people, are all different, and some dislike the responsibilities of supervising a class, and try to offload these on to the student counsellor. This includes such tasks as gathering information on students who are absent although apparently not ill, examining students' attendance records and the position of those at risk of failing, and dealing with cases of bullying. The supervising teacher should be the first person to be in contact with the student; advice from the counsellor may be sought if a problem arises within the counsellor's field of responsibility. The counsellor must clearly define the boundaries of responsibility in this manner. The school administration must define the responsibilities of supervising teachers. The counsellor cannot deal with students' complaints with regard to individual teachers except in a very limited way; such complaints are redirected to the head of teaching and the school administration.

The student counsellor is not involved in discipline problems in classes, nor in the routine monitoring of students. This is the task of the school administration. The counsellor is only involved if counselling is required in such cases.

Cases arise in which teachers call the counsellor at home about individual students who are ill or in danger of failing. Counsellors must make up their own mind on about receiving such calls outside work. It is important to confine such demands to truly serious matters, and in other cases ask the person to make contact at work.

The counsellor holds information sessions for teachers on drugs, learning difficulties, procedures in student counselling, and on studies carried out in the school in connection with counselling.

Counselling and administrators

The student counsellor is not a part of the school's administrative system. The counsellor provides advice to school administrators about groups of students and individuals.

The student counsellor who heads the counselling service attends meetings of department heads. The counsellor meets with school administrators to speak of the students, and to inform them of problems of individual students, and to negotiate exemptions and allowances if necessary due to illness. The counsellor draws up schedules on how a student's problems should be dealt with, and participates in the drafting of plans for response to trauma, to problems of individuals in classes and to bullying. The counsellor also takes part in the reviewing of objectives of the supervising teacher, collaboration with parents, and other matters concerning student welfare. If such plans are not in existence, the counsellor may prepare them and submit them to school administration for consideration. The student counsellor takes part in policy-making work, along with administrators and teachers. This includes, for instance, the creation of policies on prevention of substance abuse, on bullying, on students who do not meet the school's academic requirements, and so on.

Experience shows that many student counsellors have difficulty in setting boundaries for their area of responsibility vis-à-vis administrators. This is a young profession, so it is of great importance to seek to clarify the professional responsibilities involved. It should always be made clear that the role of the student counsellor is to be a spokesperson for the students.

CHAPTER 4

Other Roles and Responsibilities of the School Counsellor

Collaboration with specialists and institutions

As mentioned in previous chapters, the counsellor collaborates with specialists such as psychologists, physicians, psychiatrists, social workers, the clergy, other student counsellors, reading therapists and counsellors to the blind. Contact with these parties is rather time-consuming, as they are often hard to reach on the telephone. The counsellor must organise a work schedule to allow for this.

In general the counsellor consults the specialist when the student is not present, but in very serious cases it may be necessary to contact the specialist during the student's counselling session. Occasionally the counsellor and specialist exchange letters on the student, and very rarely they may meet. The counsellor's consultation with specialists is always with the knowledge and consent of the student. The objectives of such work have been discussed above.

The counsellor has contact with such institutions as the University of Education Reading Centre, the Library for the Blind, social services, hospitals, casualty departments, schools, student loan authorities and workplaces. The counsellor is in constant touch with some of these institutions all year round, with others only occasionally. Considerable collaboration takes place with social services over financial support for students, and with the Reading Centre regarding diagnosis of reading disabilities.

In general, collaboration with specialists and institutions is excellent, but on occasion the counsellor may have to exert considerable pressure on the student's behalf, so that the student receives the attention or service required. If the counsellor sees the role as that of an unconditional spokesperson for the students, it will not be hard to deal with such parties. The counsellor may have to approach the same bodies more than once on the same issue, and thus it is important to keep good records, for example noting who was spoken to and when. Follow-up is often required in some form, and maintaining organised procedures helps make this possible.

Research

Student counsellors are always kept busy, and so it is important to organise one's time well. Time must be allowed for an important aspect of the work – research, and participation in surveys carried out within the school (e.g. by the social studies department). Final-year students at Sund High School carry out various surveys, and this provides the opportunity to ask questions about study counselling and personal counselling. The school itself also carries out surveys, and this offers the same opportunity. It is of course important to examine the results of such surveys carefully, thus learning more about the students' environment.

University students of student counselling and social work carry out assignments and studies relating to the life and work of people in society. Many of these studies produce interesting results, which are stimulating for the counsellor, and generate ideas that can be applied in practice. For example the 'School counsellors' referral systems' by Jóna Rut Gudmundsdóttir clarified the complicated process a student had to go through when referred to a psychiatric ward in one of Reykjavik's hospitals. As a counsellor I had a feeling that when I referred students to the hospital they went once or didn't go at all. The study showed that when referred to the hospital only 40 per cent of students turned up but when referred to a private specialist, psychologist, 75 per cent turned up and kept in touch with the specialist. The result was that the hospital simplified its procedure.

In recent years, I have supervised work-training of five fourth-year students of social work at the University of Iceland. One aspect of their studies is to carry out research relating to their work-training, under the supervision of the work-training supervisor and tutors at the university. I have chosen the study projects, and supervised the students on methodology. Most of these students have presented their findings to meetings of teachers at Sund High School (see box).

UNIVERSITY OF ICELAND STUDENT STUDY PROJECTS SUPERVISED BY THE AUTHOR

Tilvísunarkerfi skólaráðgjafa [School counsellors' referral systems], Jóna Rut Guðmundsdóttir 1993.

Samskipti í fjölskyldum [Communication in families], Guðbjörg Hermannsdóttir 1994.

Viðhorf fjögurra nemenda til ráðgjafa [Four students' attitudes to counsellors], Anna Steinunn Ólafsdóttir 1995.

Vinna nemanda samhliða námi [Students' paid employment], Stefán Hallgrímsson 1996.

Hugmyndir nemendaí framhaldsskóla um eigið fjölskyldulíf í framtíðinni [High-school students' ideas on their own family life in the future], Björk Erlendsdóttir 1997.

N.B. These are all qualitative studies, with the exception of that on students' paid employment, which is quantitative.

Students of student counselling have also carried out many other surveys and smaller projects not listed here. All this work carried out by students of counselling contributes to clarifying knowledge of the circumstances of students in high school, and their ideas.

Ongoing education

Various courses are available for student counsellors. In Iceland courses are offered for instance by the Association of Student Counsellors, and at the University of Iceland Ongoing Education Institute. Private organisations also organise courses and government ministries hold meetings. It is vital for every working counsellor to make the best possible use of courses. This will foster a sense of professionalism, add to knowledge, improve effective working, and help avoid isolation.

It is also important that the counsellor keep notes on what was learned on the course, and produce a handy summary. Such notes, if kept in an organised fashion, will gradually form a useful handbook that can be applied to the counsellor's work. Notes and summaries can also be distributed to other counsellors and to teachers, to improve their knowledge and information.

Reading books in the field is a part of the counsellor's work. Every school has its library, and it is important to keep up with publications of new books and periodicals that would be a useful addition to the library. The counsellor must allow time for reading, and other gathering of information, for instance on the internet.

Information gathering is an important factor, which must be carried out regularly, so that the counsellor always has the latest information on research, studies and new methods of working at her disposal.

Student counsellors must keep up with new developments in methods, for example quality-control methods, and other approaches that may be used to improve the effectiveness of counselling, while also being conducive to development in the profession, and giving the counsellor new ideas to work with. The study by Stefán Hallgrímsson 'Students' paid employment' showed that we had inaccurate ideas about how many hours students needed to work as well as studying, and that girls worked more hours than boys. Another study, 'High-school students' ideas on their own family life in the future' by Björk Erlensdóttir showed that students were more conservative than we thought. They liked the 'old family values' in , for example, the upbringing of their children.

Supervision

Those whose work involves close personal interaction, dealing with sensitive personal issues, require regular and effective guidance, if they are to avoid exhaustion and premature burn-out. Supervision is useful in evaluating one's own work, as counsellors often carry out their work without consultation with other counsellors – and it increases professional awareness. Counsellors who are starting out should study the procedures of older and more experienced colleagues, and should have their own methods evaluated. Many cases facing student counsellors are difficult and demanding, such as suicide risk, violence, depression, eating disorders, psychological trauma and children at risk. In such cases supervision must be available. The counsellor must give good advice, and this is best achieved by not overestimating one's own competence or ability, while being able to work through distressing cases under supervision.

The counsellor goes to a psychologist, social worker or colleague once a week or once a month for supervision on their work. They can take questions about special problems they come across in their work and for supervision on the effect the work has on their personal life.

Counsellors must be able to provide colleagues with supervision, when they have gained experience and established themselves. In order to provide supervision, it is important to have received guidance. Courses for those who wish to provide supervision to others in their work are a useful option for most counsellors.

Group work

Group work is useful for certain purposes, but has undeniable limitations. The objective of group work should not be to save time or money. The purpose of counselling is to help individuals define their problems and deal with them. Work with students must thus primarily serve the individual.

Group work is not suitable in cases of individual problems, such as low self-esteem, isolation, examination anxiety, and so on, unless it is ensured that regular individual counselling sessions take place while group work is in progress.

Five is a suitable size of group. Group work is useful for the following purposes:

- to educate a group on a subject through assignments, e.g. on substance abuse or legal rights

- to practise certain methods – study technique, drawing up of work schedules, setting of objectives, etc.

- to improve understanding of circumstances, e.g. bullying, disabilities, financial difficulties

- to identify shared needs of students, and different needs of male and female students

- to create support groups for students, e.g. students with reading difficulties or other comparable problems that hinder them in their studies.

Work-training for university students

One aspect of the counsellor's work is work-training for students of counselling at the university who are studying to become school counsellors or social workers. They all have to spend a learning period with a qualified supervisor at work. Work-training varies in duration, but is usually not more than 100 hours. The period should be viewed as a whole and organised as such. It is a good idea to divide the period into three phases, each with its own theme – such as counselling technique, the imbalance of power between client and counsellor, and writing reports – clarifying the training involved in each theme. The following framework may be used:

- The institution/school, staff and facilities are introduced.

- The student receives a list of possible research projects, and chooses one in consultation with the job-training supervisor.

- The division of the training period is discussed on the three-theme basis.

- Evaluation interviews are carried out and the student is prepared for receiving criticism in a positive way.

- The student and teacher discuss their expectations. The teacher sets out standards regarding attendance, confidentiality and other key aspects of training.

- The teacher arranges for the student to be an observer at a number of counselling sessions at first, in which the student is expected to bring together theory and practice. This is to be done by observing the teacher's approach in counselling sessions, and discussing it afterwards. The student then gives counselling in the presence of the teacher, and practises especially those aspects criticised by the teacher. Finally, the student takes counselling sessions alone, making audio recordings of several sessions (2–4), with the client's consent. The teacher then listens to the tapes with the student. This is followed by discussion of the student's growing skill, or lack of progress, or other matters.

- The imbalance of power between client and counsellor must always be at the back of the counsellor's mind. This concept has to be emphasised in the sessions. The teacher observes with this in mind and points out weaknesses in the counselling of the student, for example the student forgets information that has been given by the client or does not take notice of how the client is conducting themself. An extreme example would be if the student constantly referred to their own experience and did not listen to the client.

- Writing reports is important because while doing that the student reviews the case, putting things in perspective and systematic order, and gains an overview of the client's situation.

- The student submits a work plan for a research project such as those referred to above (pp.72–73).

The student counsellor's expertise

Student counsellors have access to the 'hidden society' of the young. They gain familiarity with a reality and ideas, that are open to few adults. The confidentiality that the counsellor promises to the student gives the counsellor this important access. This privileged knowledge is in my view undervalued. The individual stories of young people give the counsellor valuable insights into young people, their views and their culture

Adults, of course, have preconceptions about young people, based mostly on their own experience and what they see. Adults try to influence the conduct and views of the young, generally with limited success. Before we can really address the problems that young people have in society (or the problems that adult society thinks it has with young people, which is not the same thing), we must include their viewpoint in the solution. A good example of this is the question of substance abuse, where there is a divergence of views between young people and their parents' generation. In sessions with students you get information about how the dealers approach the students and what kind of substances are in use at the moment. You also learn about the propaganda used to persuade the students to 'try', and information about the 'hottest' places, for example discos etc.

Unfortunately, too little use is made of student counsellors' expertise. Four reasons for this may be mentioned:

- Counsellors do not necessarily realise that they have this unusual expertise, and they undervalue it.

- Counsellors who attempt to apply this expertise in the interests of the student are not listened to by administrators, teachers or the public, as the information tends to be fragmentary.

- The information that counsellors possess is often highly negative toward 'conventional society', and may even be perceived as threatening. Counsellors tend to reject such information, or even erase it completely from their minds.

- Overwork, together with the pressure of working very closely with individuals and their personal problems, tends to lead to burn-out in counsellors. They lose faith in the value of what they are doing, and may decide to change over to another field of work, or simply coast through the retirement.

It is not an easy task to draw up the outlines of the 'hidden society', but it is to be hoped that counsellors will join forces to establish a store of knowledge that will make a difference to young people, and be conducive to a better life for them. Improvements must be based on information that comes from the 'inside', not on ideas based on fragmentary premises. This applies to such matters as substance abuse, violence, sexual abuse, poverty, loneliness, suicide, bullying, and anxiety. All these problems are of grave importance, and may be matters of life and death.

The matters mentioned above are the darker aspects of the case. But there are two sides to most questions. Young people also provide constructive information on improvements they would like to see, for example on new teaching methods, more productive study methods, group support, more effective study assessment, shorter duration of studies, with less attendance at school and more independent study, and a more friendly school environment.

Parents are busy, earning a living to support their family. They do not always have enough time for full participation in their children's lives. The counsellor's expertise is an important means of bridging the gap between adults and young people. But counsellors must not become entirely caught up in the day-to-day work of counselling. They must take ethical responsibility for their expertise, and make use of it for good purposes.

Bibliography

Anorexia nervosa og bulimia nervosa; teori og behandling (1985). Bergen: Universitetsforlaget.

Ársskýrsla Rauðakrosshússins [Annual Report of Red Cross Young People's Refuge] (1996) Reykjavík: Rauði kross Íslands.

Ársskýrsla S.Á.Á. [Annual Report of the National Centre of Addiction Medicine] (1996). Reykjavík: S.Á.Á.

Ársskýrsla Félagsmálastofnunar í Reykjavík [Annual Report of Reykjavík Social Services] (1996). Reykjavík: Reykjavíkurborg.

Björnsson, Sigurjón (1983) *Sálkönnun og sállækningar: nokkrir þættir* [Psychoanalysis and psychotherapy: some aspects]. Reykjavík: Bókmenntafélagið.

Burks, H. M. and Stefflre, B. (1979) *Theories of Counseling*, 3rd. ed. USA: McGraw-Hill.

Carlson, J. and Lewis, J. (1993) *Counseling the Adolescent: individual, family and school interventions.* Denver: Love.

Cox, M. (1988) *Structuring the Therapeutic Process: compromise with chaos.* London: Jessica Kingsley.

Davey, G. and Tallis, F. (1994) *Worrying: perspectives on theory, assessment and treatment.* New York: Wiley.

Erlendsdóttir, B. (1997) *Hugmyndir nemenda í framhaldsskóla um eigið fjölskyldulíf í framtíðinni* [High-school students' ideas on their own family life in the future]. Unpublished dissertation, University of Iceland.

Finset, A. (1988) *Familien og det social netværket* [The family and the social network]. Oslo: J. W. Cappelans Forlag.

Gersie, A. (1996) *Storymaking in Bereavement: dragons fight in the meadow.* London: Jessica Kingsley.

Gordon, T. (2000) *P.E.T. Parent Effectiveness Training: the proven program for raising responsible children.* USA: Three Rivers Press.

Guðmundsdóttir, J.R. (1993) *Tilvísanakerfi skólaráðgjafa* [School counsellors' referral systems]. Unpublished dissertation, University of Iceland.

Gut, E. (1989) *Den gode depression. Fölelsesforlob, behandling og personlighedsudvikling* [The Good Depression: evolution of feelings, therapy and personal development]. Copenhagen: Hans Reitzels Forlag.

Hallgrímsson, S. (1996) *Vinna nemenda samhliða námi* [Students' paid employment]. Unpublished dissertation, University of Iceland.

Heap, K. (1988) *Om processed I socialt arbeid med grupper* [Developments in Social Work with Groups]. Copenhagen: Munksgaard.

Helgason, L. (1996) *Kvíði: leiðbeiningar fyrir sjúklinga og aðstandendur* [Anxiety: guidelines for patients and their relatives]. Hafnarfjörður: Delta.

Helgason, L. (1996) *Þunglyndi: leiðbeiningar fyrir sjúklinga og aðstandendur* [Depression: guidelines for patients and their relatives]. Hafnarfjörður: Delta.

Helgason, L. (1996): *Geðklofi: leiðbeiningar fyrir sjúklinga og aðstandendur* [Schizophrenia: guidelines for patients and their relatives]. Hafnarfjörður: Delta.

Hermannsdóttir, G.E. (1994) *Samskipti í fjölskyldum* [Communication in families]. Unpublished dissertation, University of Iceland.

Hillgaard, L. and Keiser, L. (1981) *Social (be)handling: Teori og metode I social arbejde* [Social Therapy: theory and practice in social work].Copenhagen: Munksgaard.

Holland, J.L. (1973) *Making Vocational Choices: a theory of careers*. Englewood Cliffs, NJ: Prentice Hall.

Ivey, A.E. (1983) *International Interviewing and Counseling*. California: Wadsworth.

Júlíusdóttir, S. (1989) *Félagsráðgjöf: rannsóknir og fagþróun* [Social counselling: research and professional development]. Reykjavík: Háskóli Íslands.

Kendall, P.C. (1995) *Abnormal Psychology*. Boston: Houghton Mifflin.

Lishman, J. (ed) (1991) *Handbook of Theory for Practice Teachers in Social Work*. London: Jessica Kingsley.

Nám á Íslandi: kynning á námi að loknum framhaldsskóla sem miðar að starfsréttindum [Study in Iceland: courses in higher education leading to professional qualifications] (1995). Reykjavík: Háskóli Íslands.

Oltmans, T.F. (1995) *Case Studies in Abnormal Psychology*. New York: Wiley.

Ólafsdóttir, A.S. (1995) *Viðhorf fjögurra nemanda til ráðgjafa* [Four students' attitudes to counsellors]. Unpublished dissertation, University of Iceland.

Oskarsdóttir, G.G. (1990) *Starfslýsingar: sérfræði, tækni- og stjórnunarstörf* [Job descriptions: specialist, technical and administrative posts] Reykjavík: Iðunn.

Patton, M. J. (1992) *Psychoanalytic Counseling*. New York: Wiley.

Rogers, C.R. (1991) *Client-Centred Therapy*. London: Redwood Press.

Ryden, M. (1997) *Dyslexia. How Would I Cope?* London: Jessica Kingsley.

Sederholm, G.H. *Ársskýrslur námsráðgjafa í Menntaskólanum við Sund* [Annual Reports of Student Counsellors at Sund High School] (1991–1997). Reykjavík: Sund High School

Sederholm, G.H.,(ed) Ragnarsdóttir, A. Arnbjörnsson, O.J., Agustsdóttir, S. And Hardardóttir, S. (1988) *Efling náms- og starfsráðgjafar* [Promotion of study and career counselling]. Committee report for the Icelandic Ministry of Education.

Staða barna á Ísland: Barnasáttmáli Sameinuðu þjóðanna [Children's Status in Iceland: the UN Convention on the Rights of the Child]. Reykjavík: Barnaheill.

Stierling, H. (1989) *Unlocking the family door: a systemic approach to the understanding and treatment of anorexia nervosa*. New York: Brummer/Mazel.

UN Children's Rights.

Vernon, A. (1993) *Counseling Children and Adolescents*. Denver: Love.

Worden, J. W. (1988) *Grief Counselling and Grief Therapy*. London: Routledge.

Index